Magic Mailer Book

by
Joyce Shearin

Materials:

pages of resume paper

pages of letter envelopes

page of stamped letter envelope sealer on adhesive paper

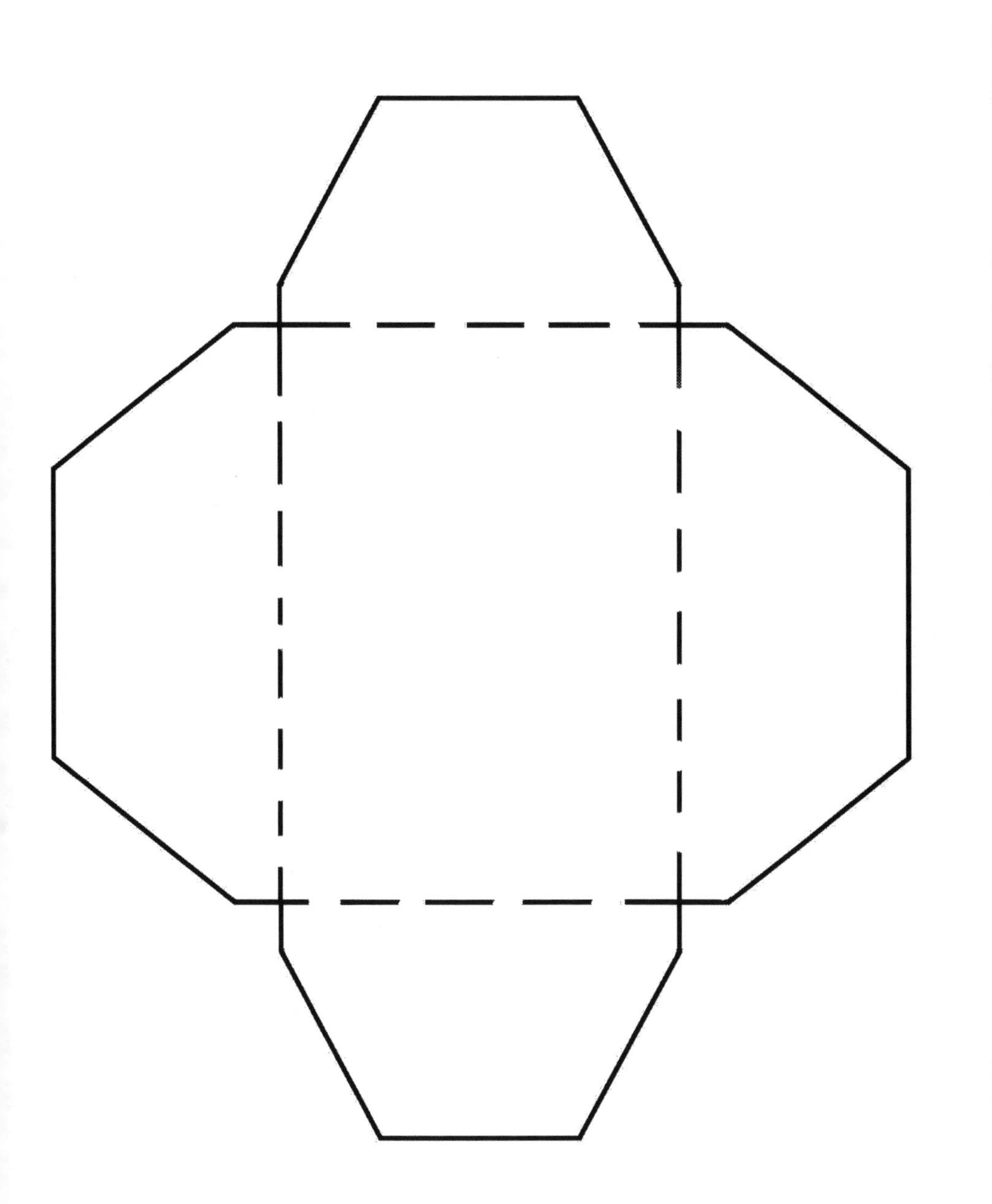

Every Second Counts,
make the most of your life.

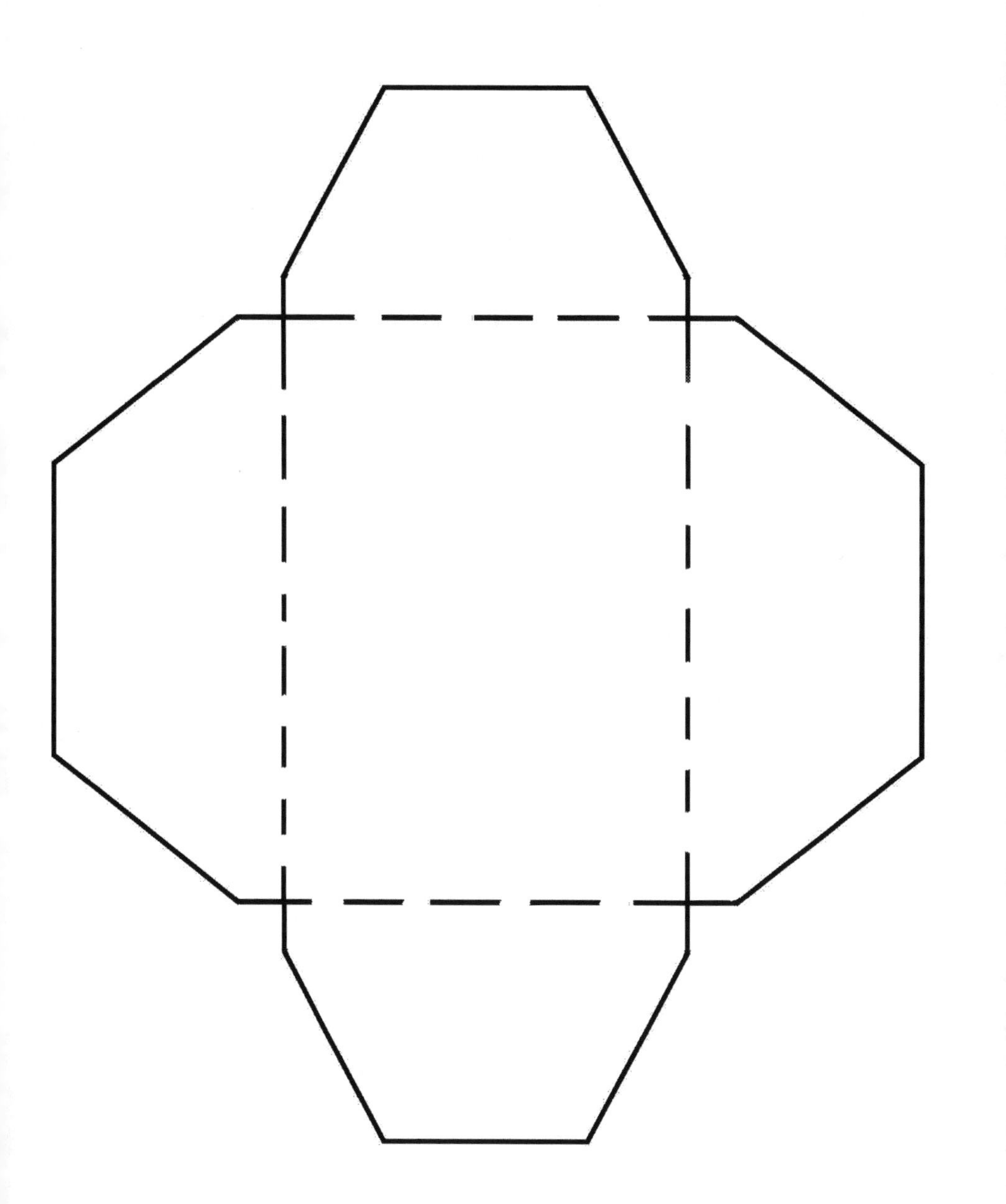

Tips To Make Extra Money

1. Convert a hobby
2. Work part-time
3. Volunteer (sometimes they might help back or tip)
4. Become an extra actor or actress
5. Start a small farm
6. Join a union (sometimes it helps)

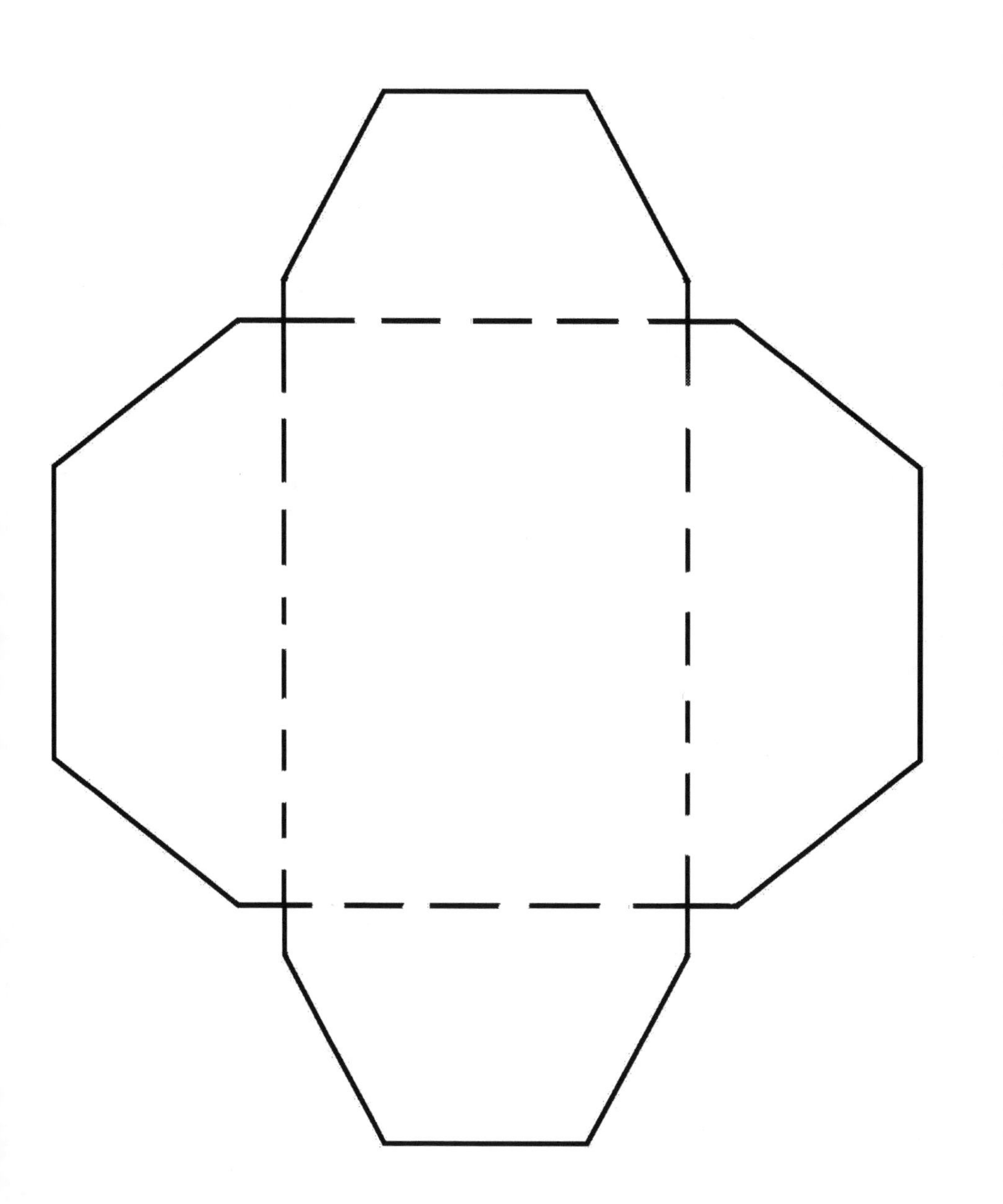

Please buy and read

Cooking Magic

By

Joyce Shearin

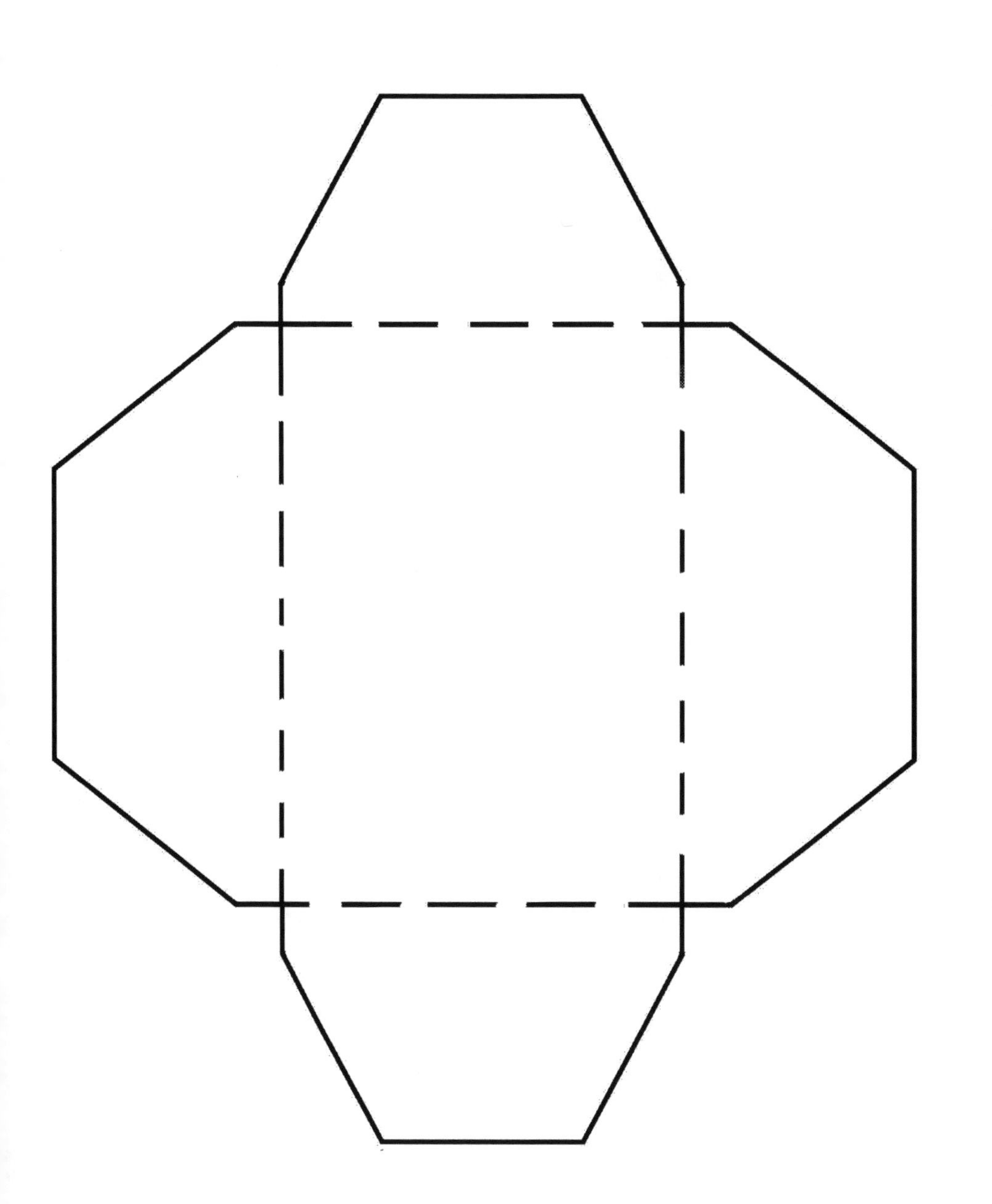

All lives Matter.

On life's Journey, take the best road.

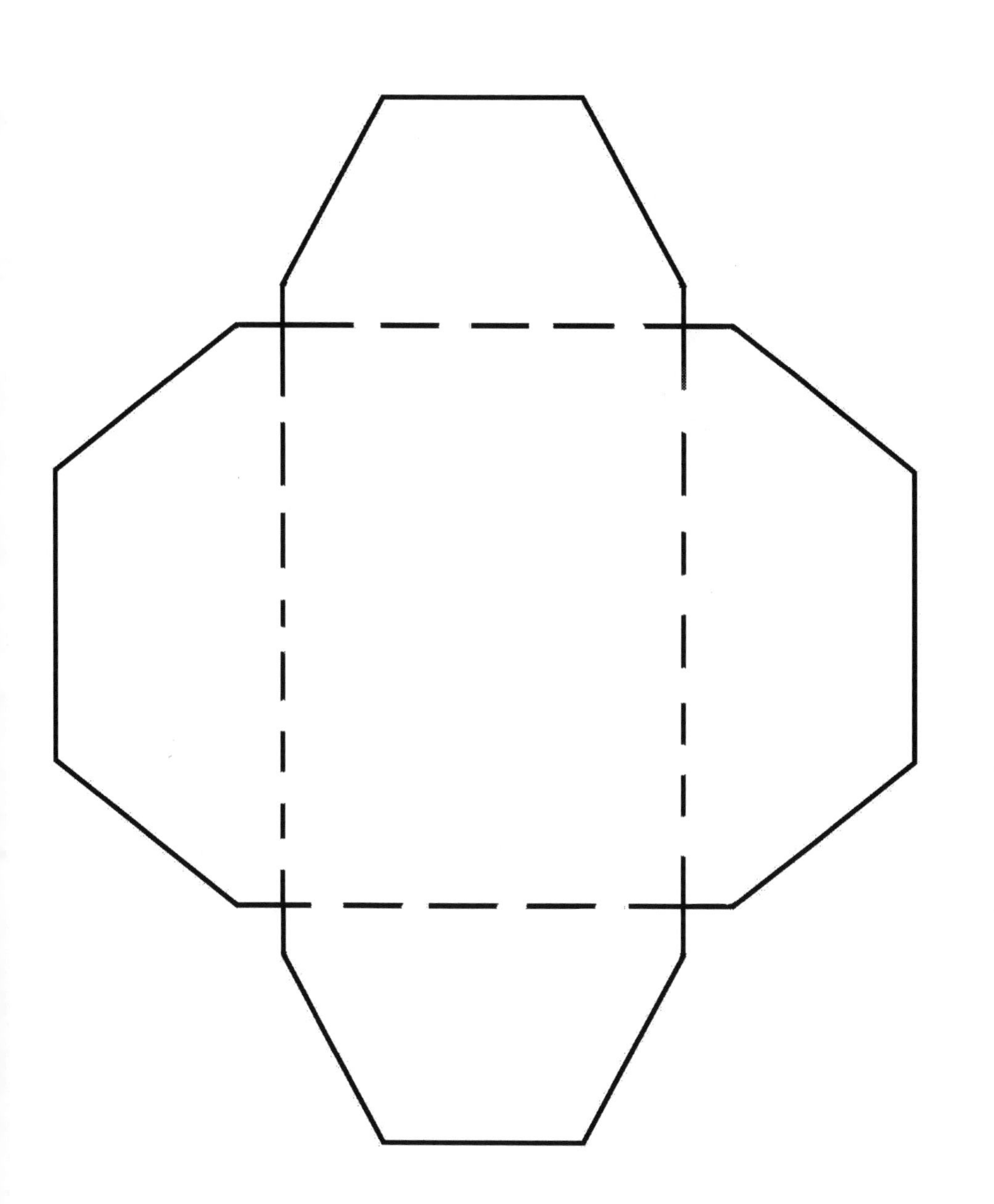

Sweet Banana Pudding

1 pkg of Nabisco wafer/cookies

1 lb bananas

1 can sweet condensed or regular milk

Add sugar to taste

Combine - wala -

Bake will ready if desired.

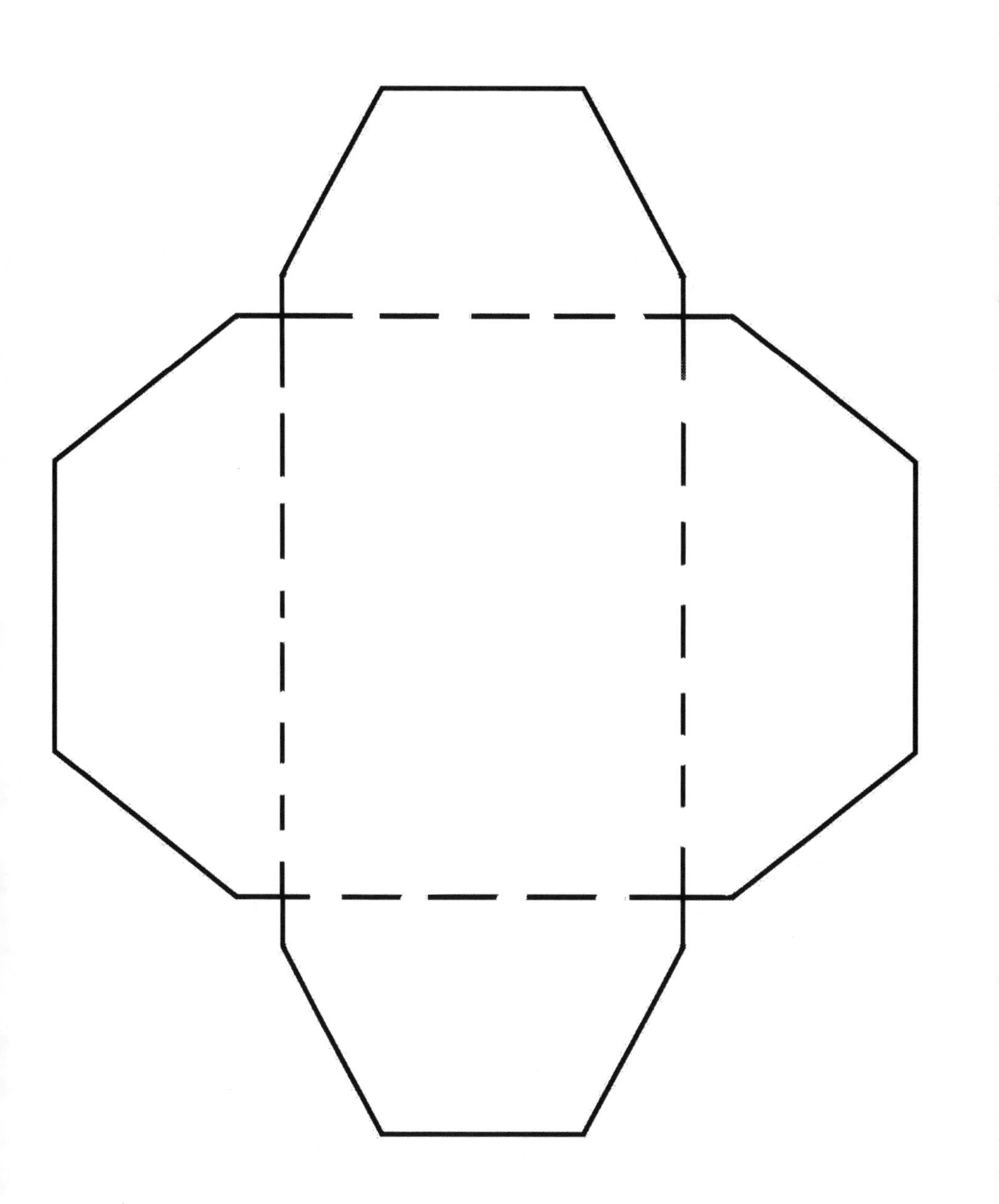

Learn, Work and enjoy!

-Joyce Shearin

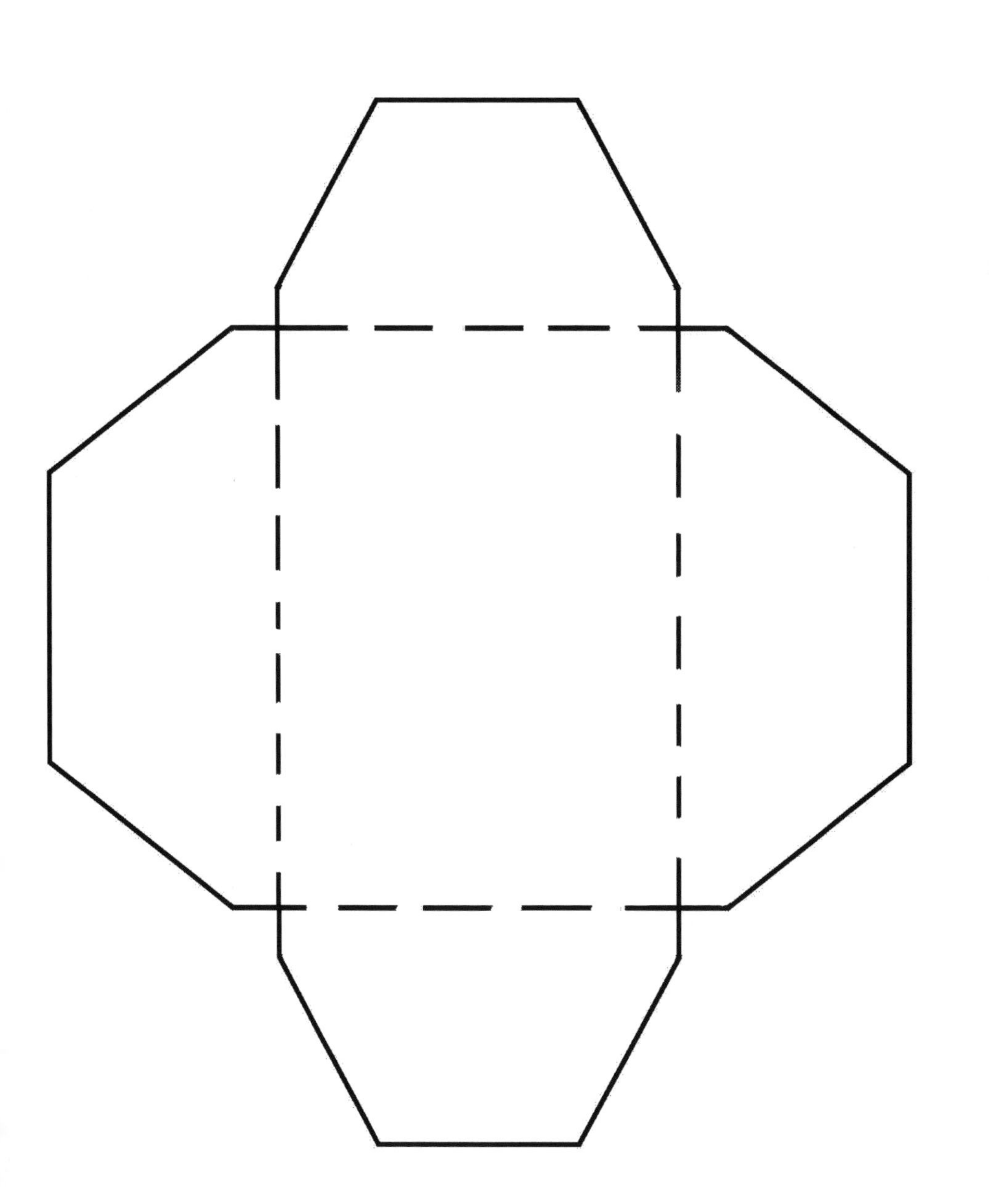

Ingredients for Miraculous Macaroni Salad

-Macaroni

-relish

-mayonnaise

-onion powder

-garlic powder

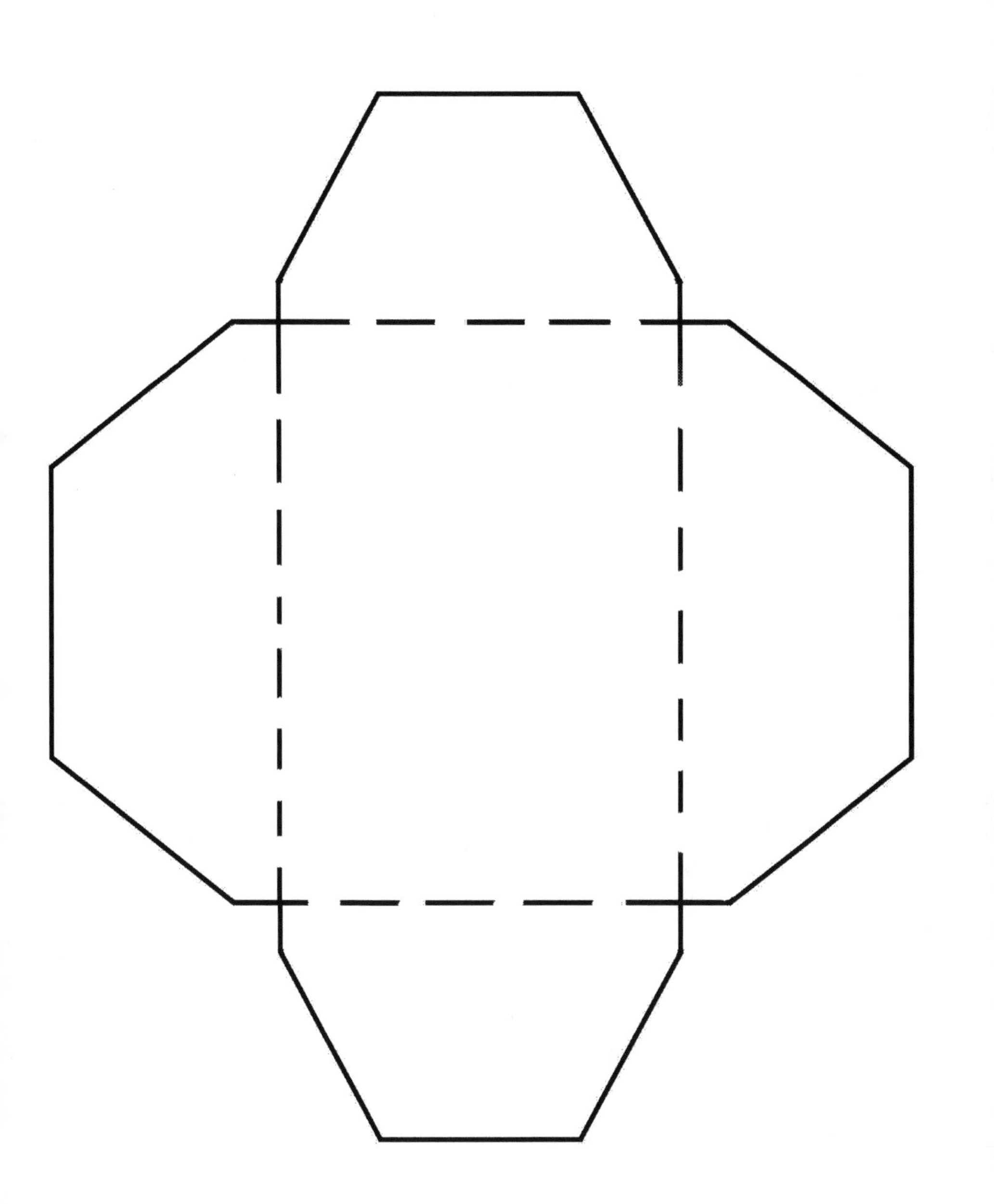

Recipe Miraculous Macaroni Salad

1. Mix Macaroni, relish and mayonnaise in the bowl
2. Add onion powder
3. Add garlic powder
4. Add any salt and seasoning to your taste
5. Enjoy!

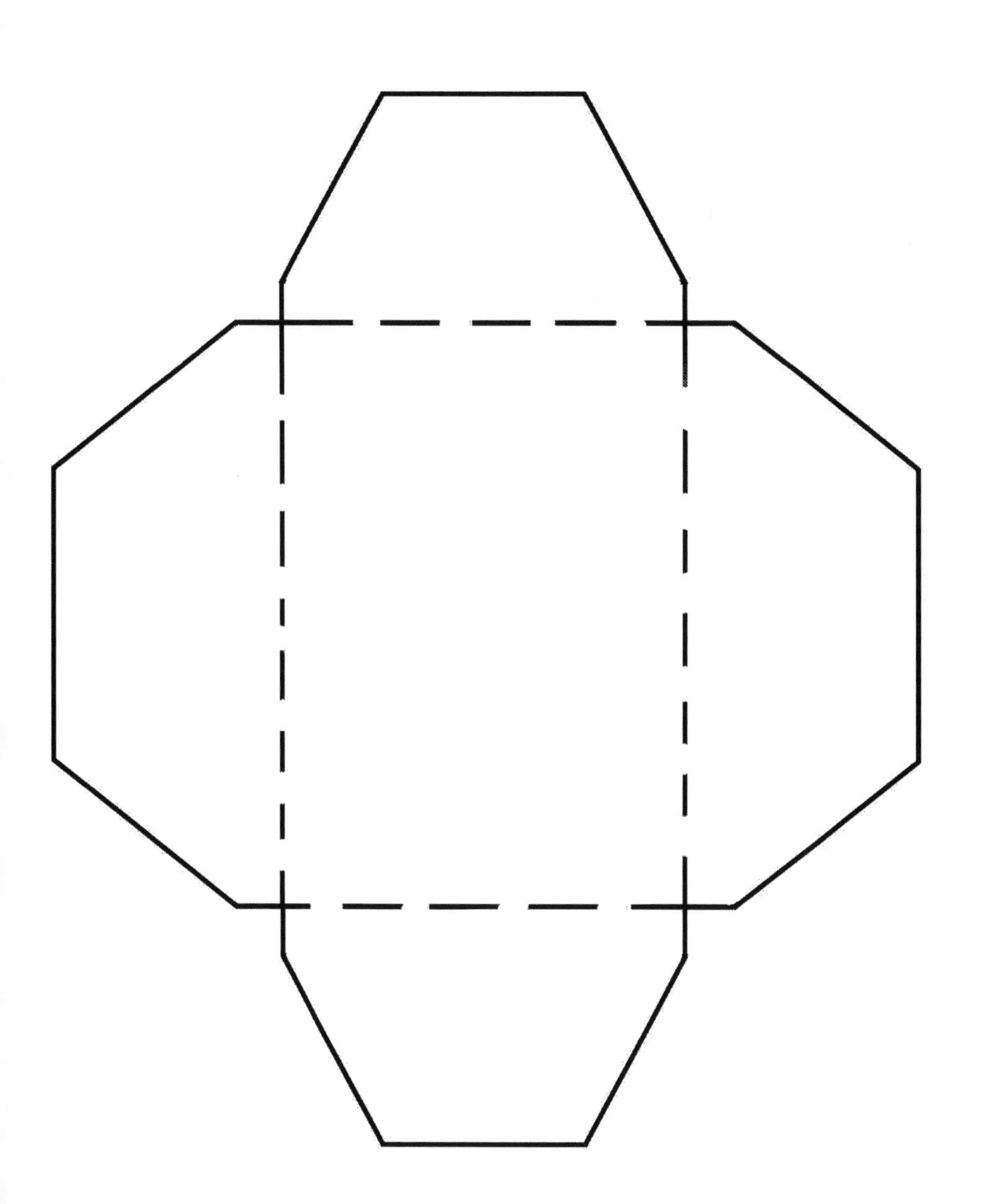

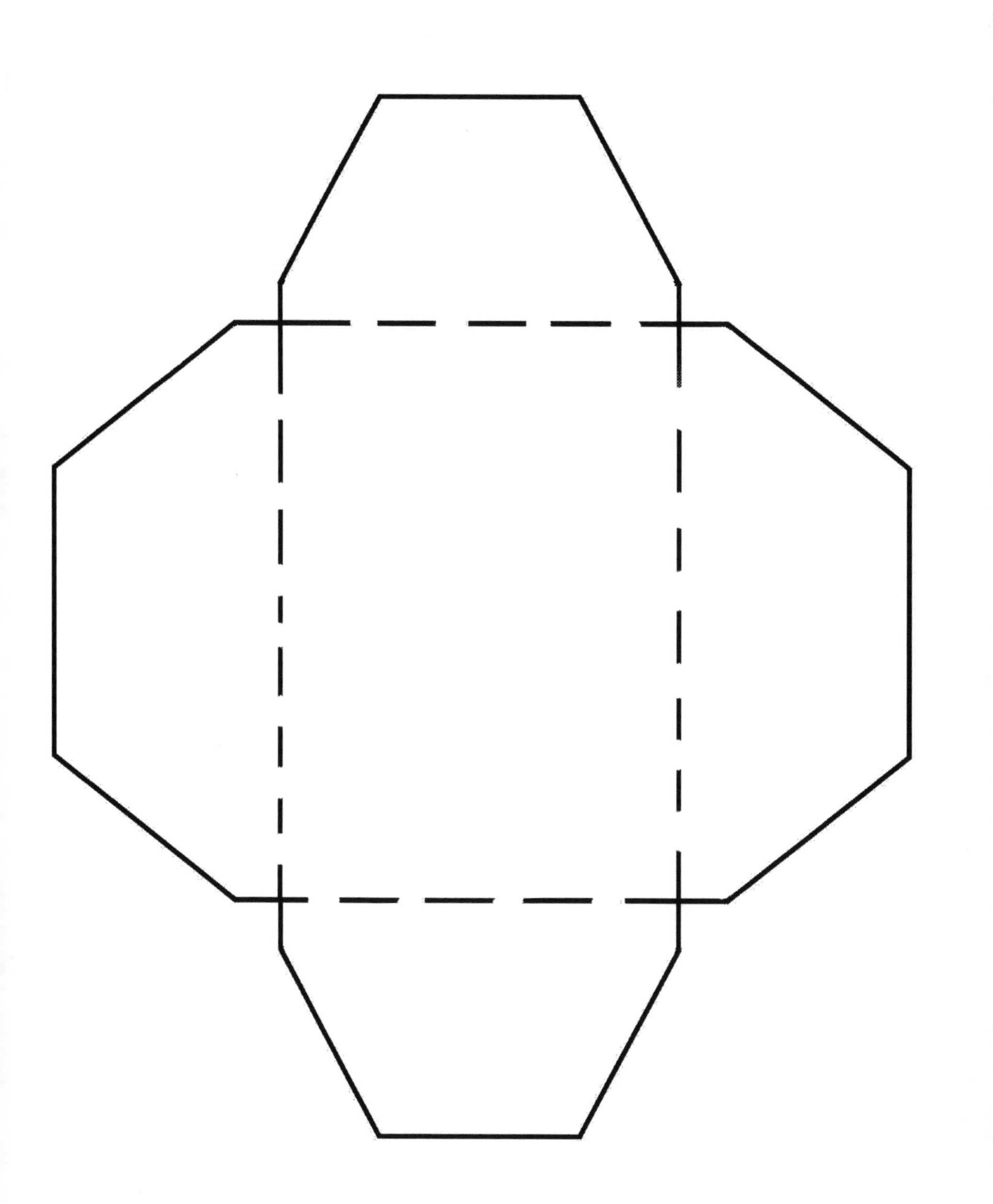

Beef/Oxtail Stew

1 lb beef cubes or 1 lb oxtail

1 8oz. can of tomato paste or stewed tomato

1 small onion

dash of salt/pepper/season salt

boil beef to taste

add tomatoes, onion and seasoning.

Simmer

Wala, there you go.

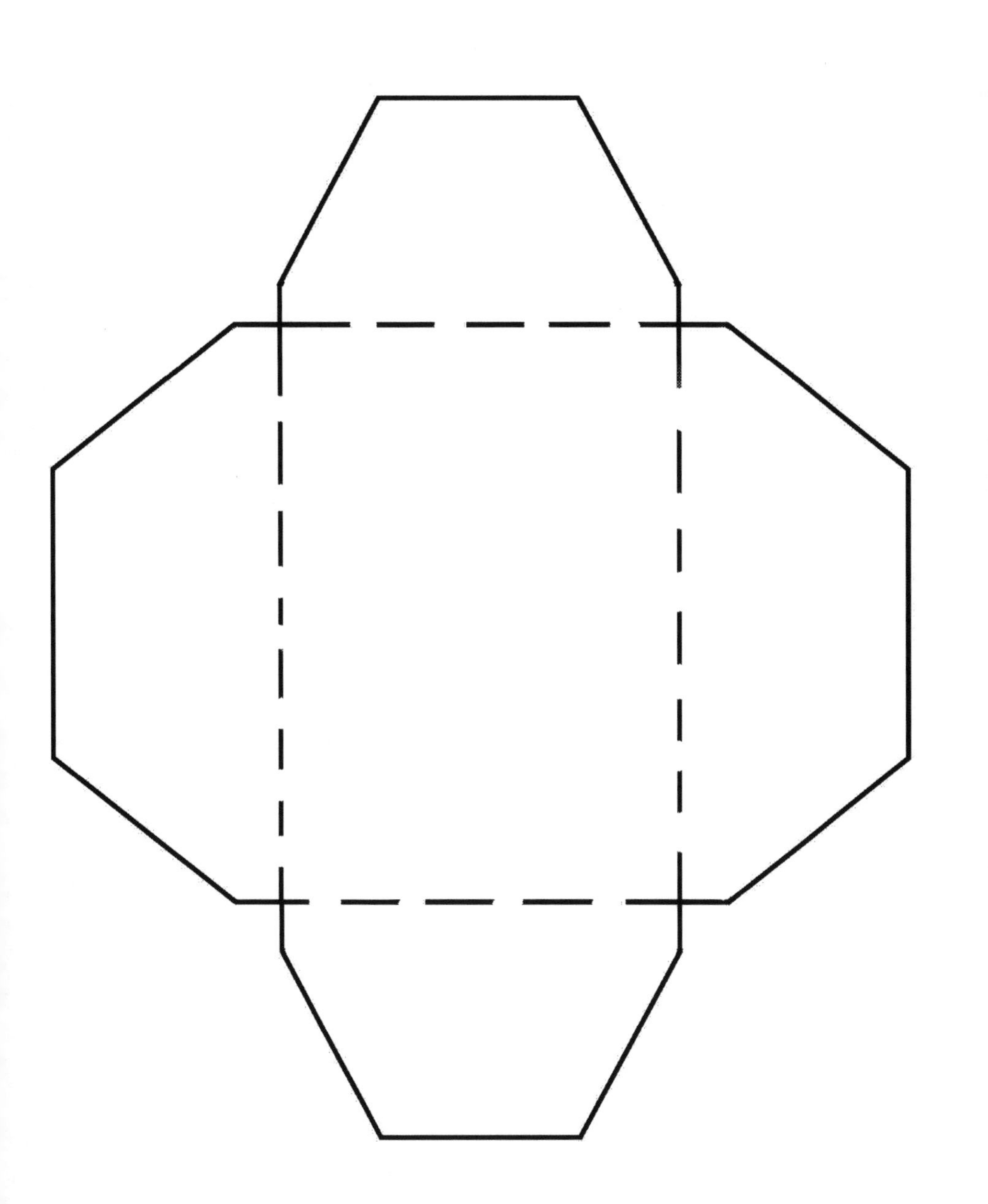

I enjoy writing and I hope to become a lawyer one day, you should also work on your dreams.

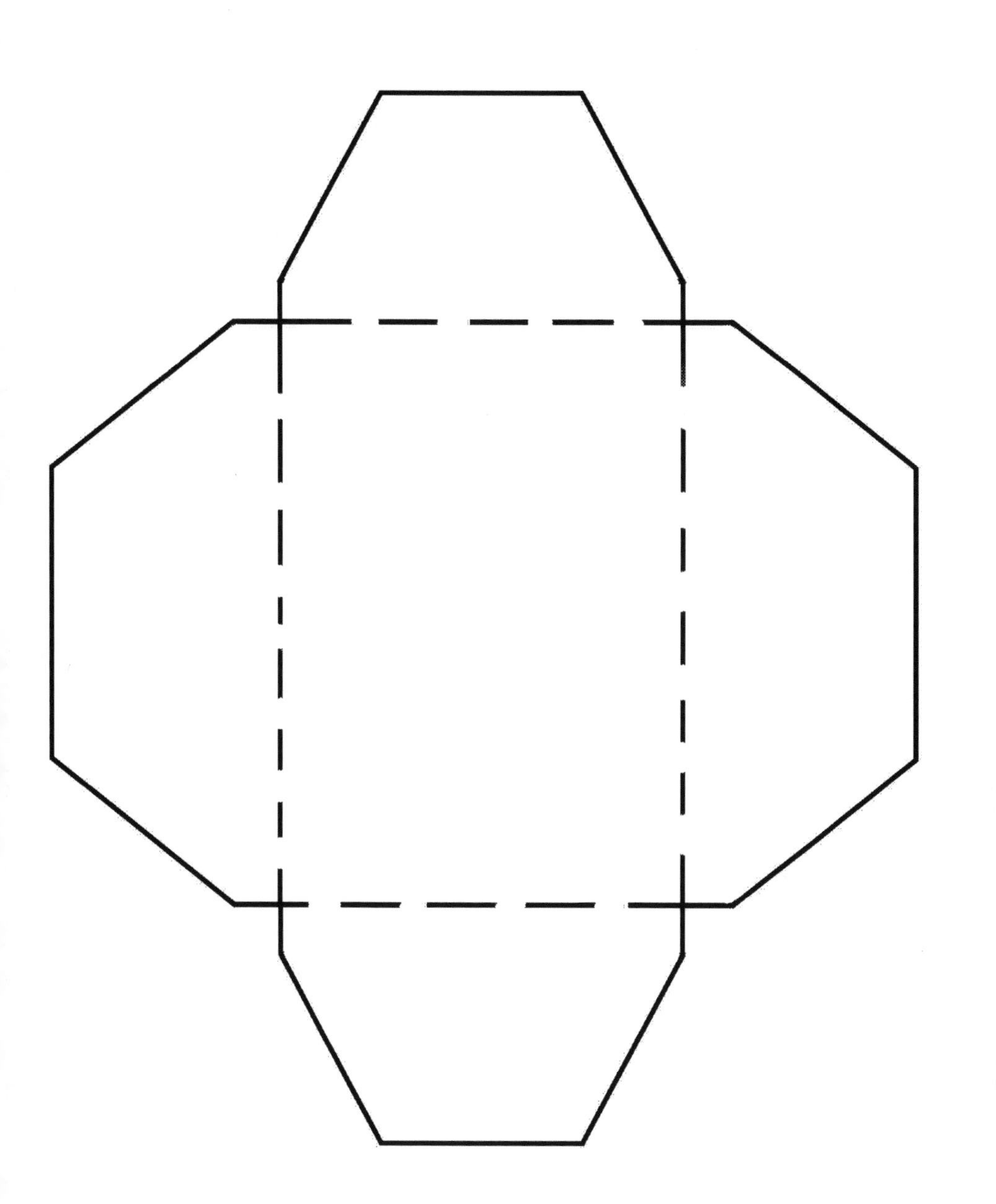

Please buy and read

Generation

By

Joyce Shearin

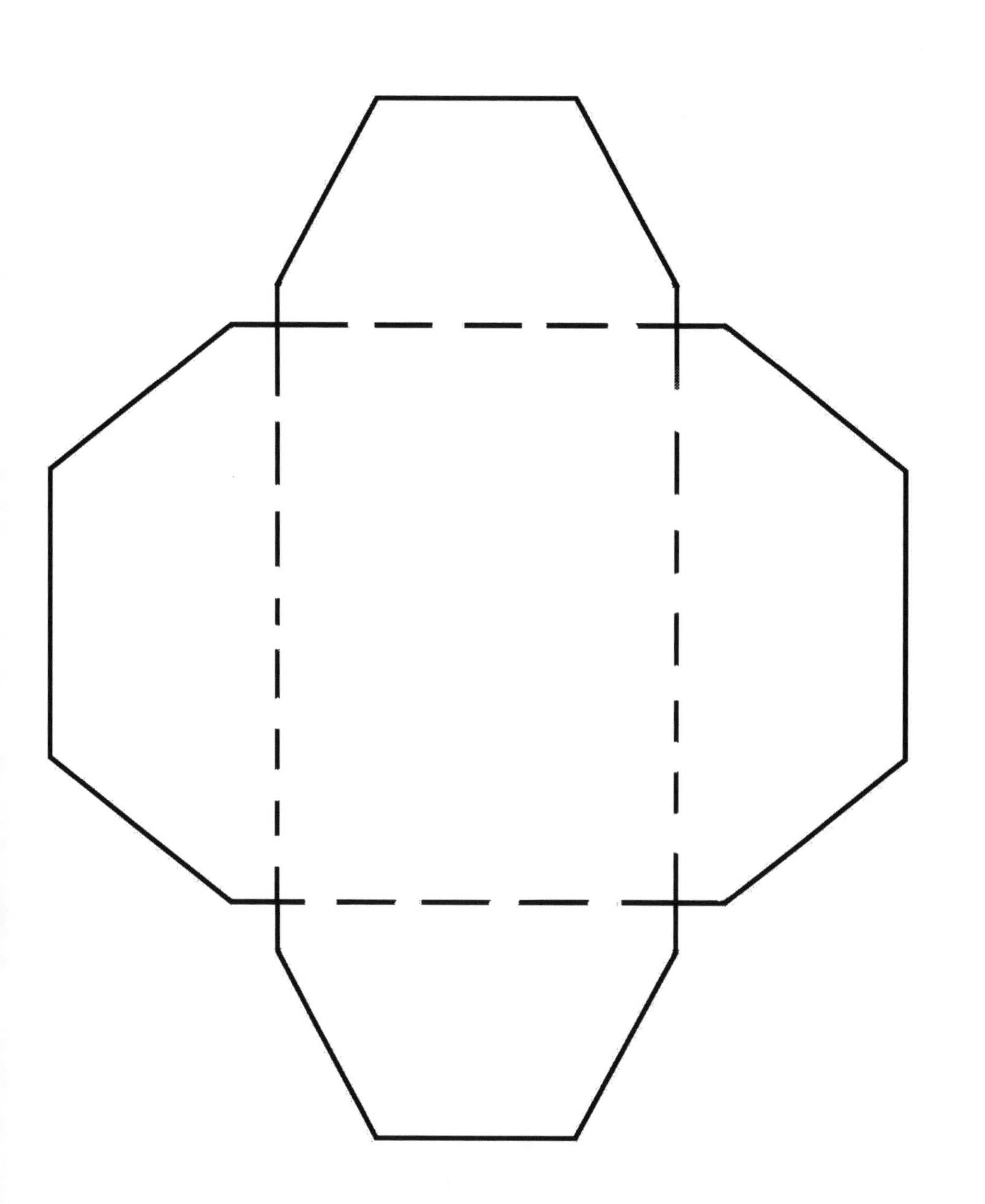

Chicken Gumbo

1 lb cooked chicken diced

1 can vegetable soup heated.

1.4 lb rice or pasta cooked if desired.

Combine above season to taste.

New Orleans style gumbo made

at home or anywhere.

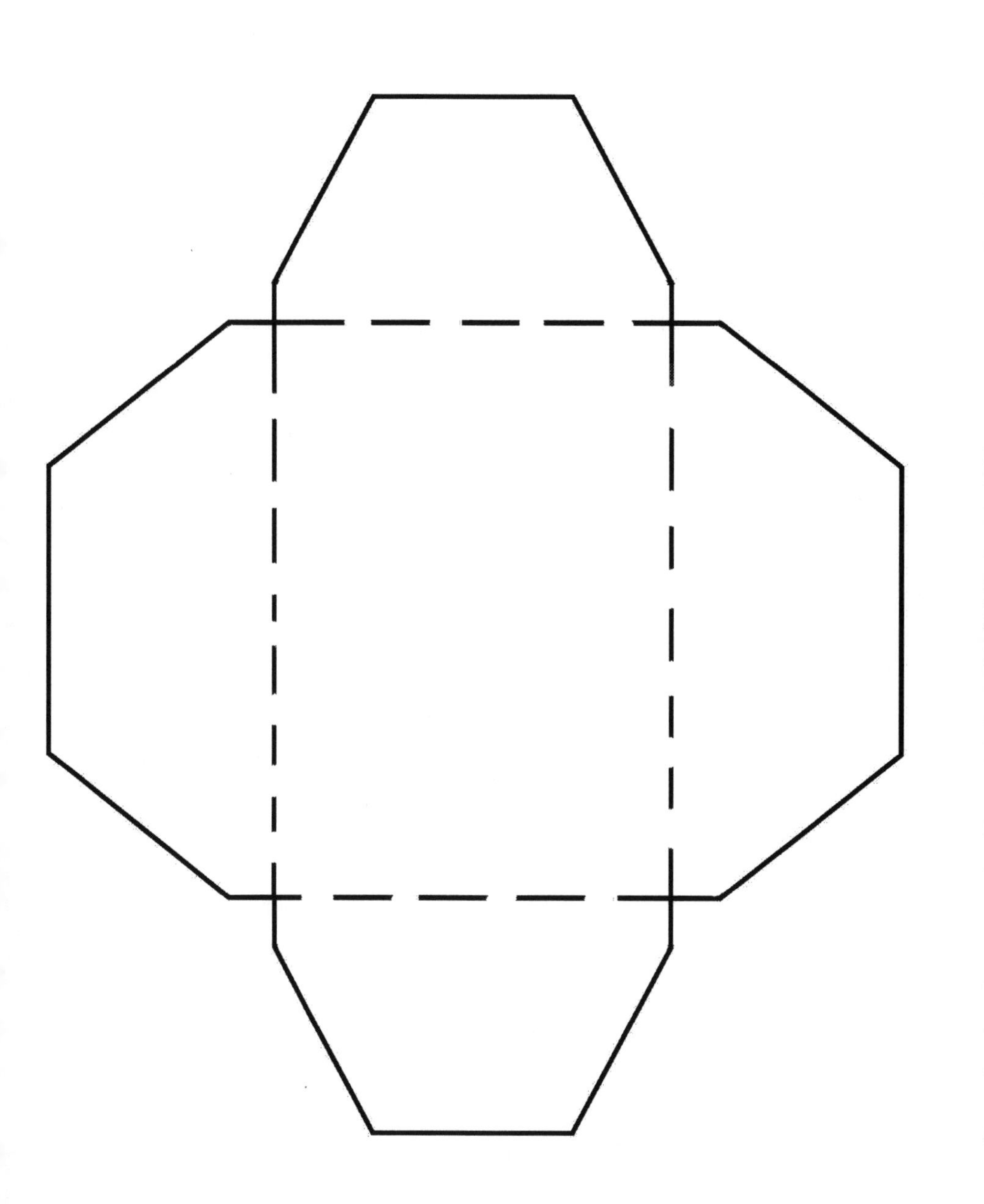

I'm hoping for the best in life for me,
for you and for everyone I love.

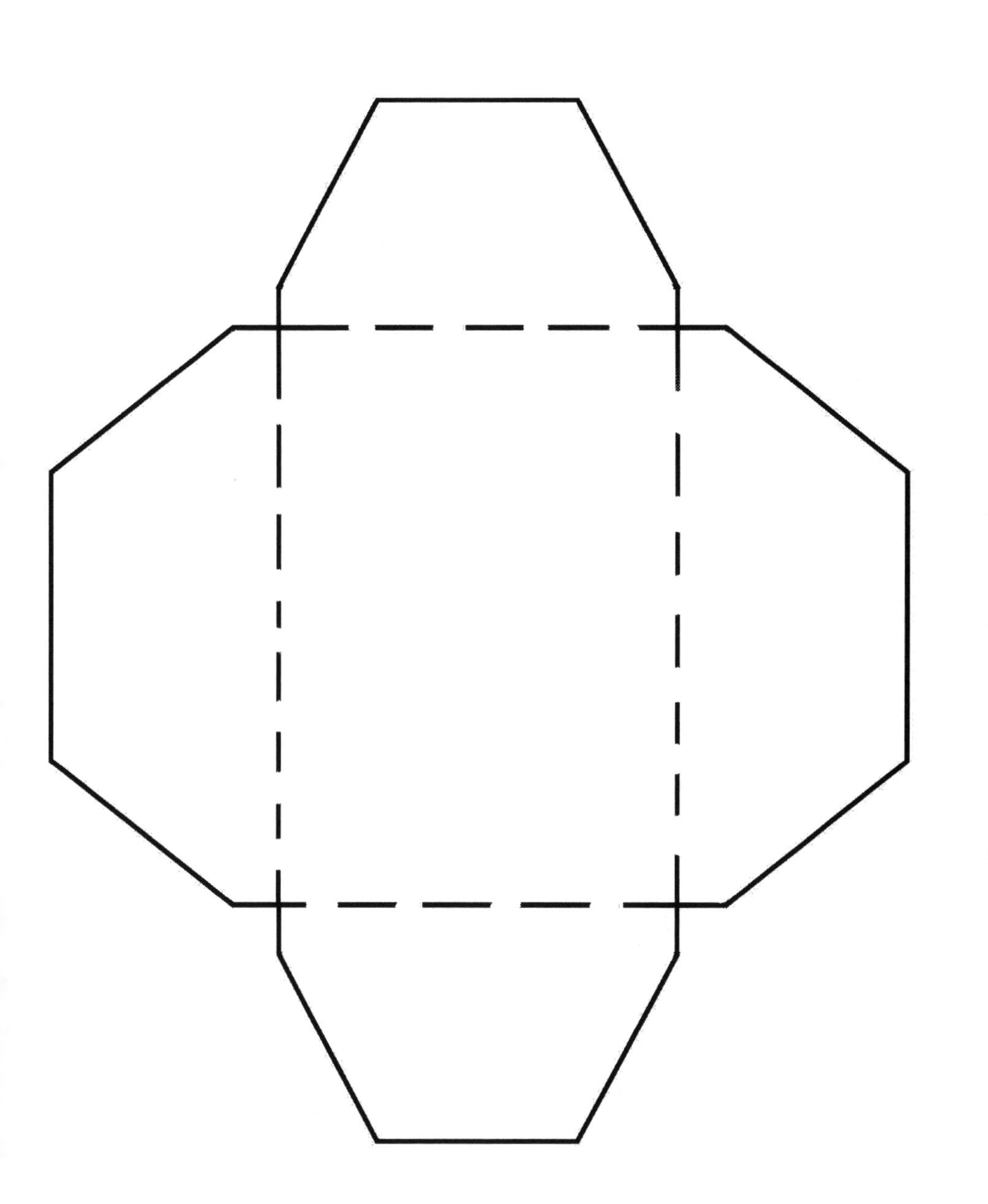

Dream Big.

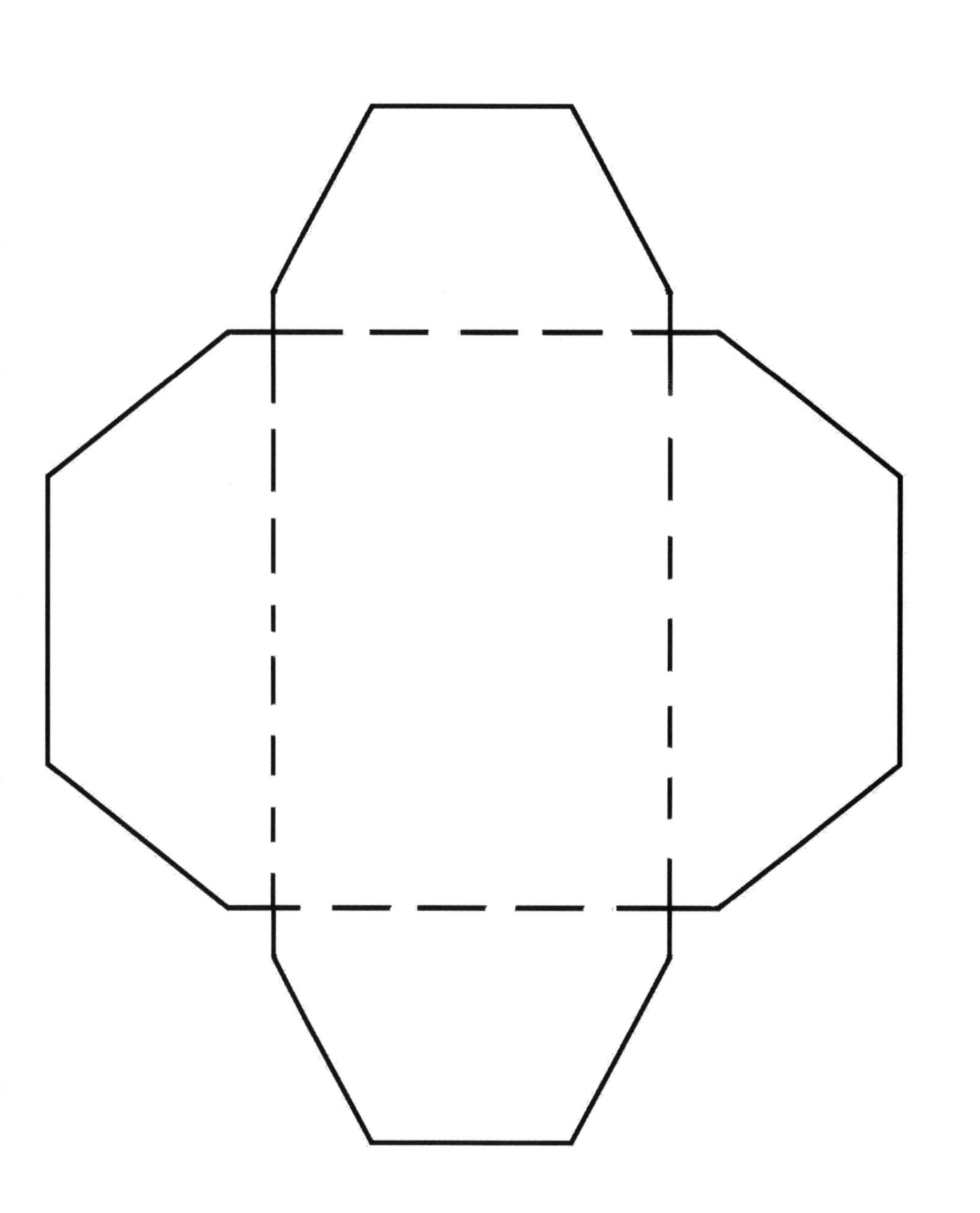

Sweet Potato Pie

2 sweet potatoes

2 eggs

1/2 cup of milk

1/4 cup of butter

1 pie crust

1/2 cup of sugar

Combine ingredients

Bake till brown.

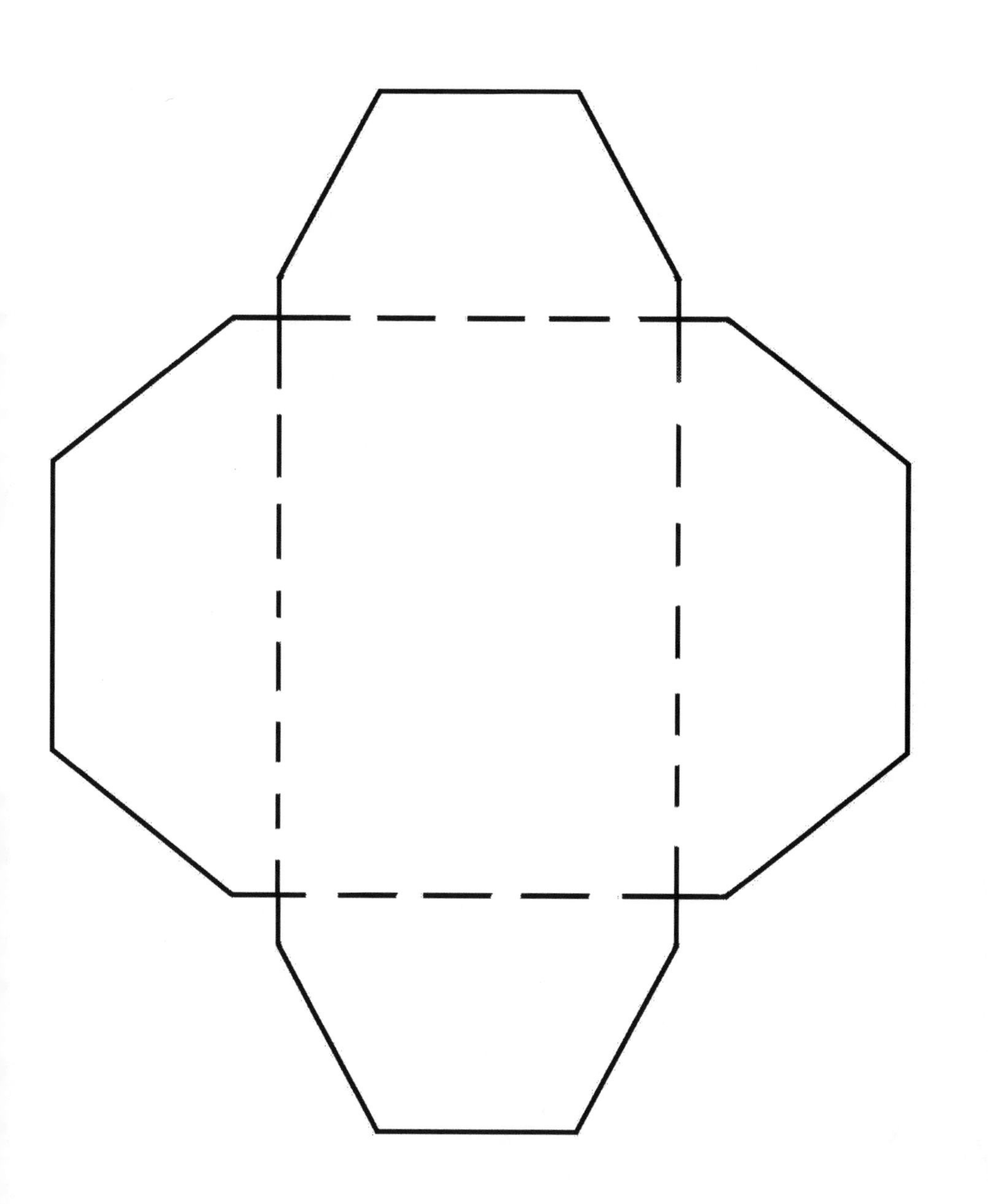

Please buy and read

BUSINESS IDEAS TO MAKE A MILLION DOLLARS

By

Joyce Shearin

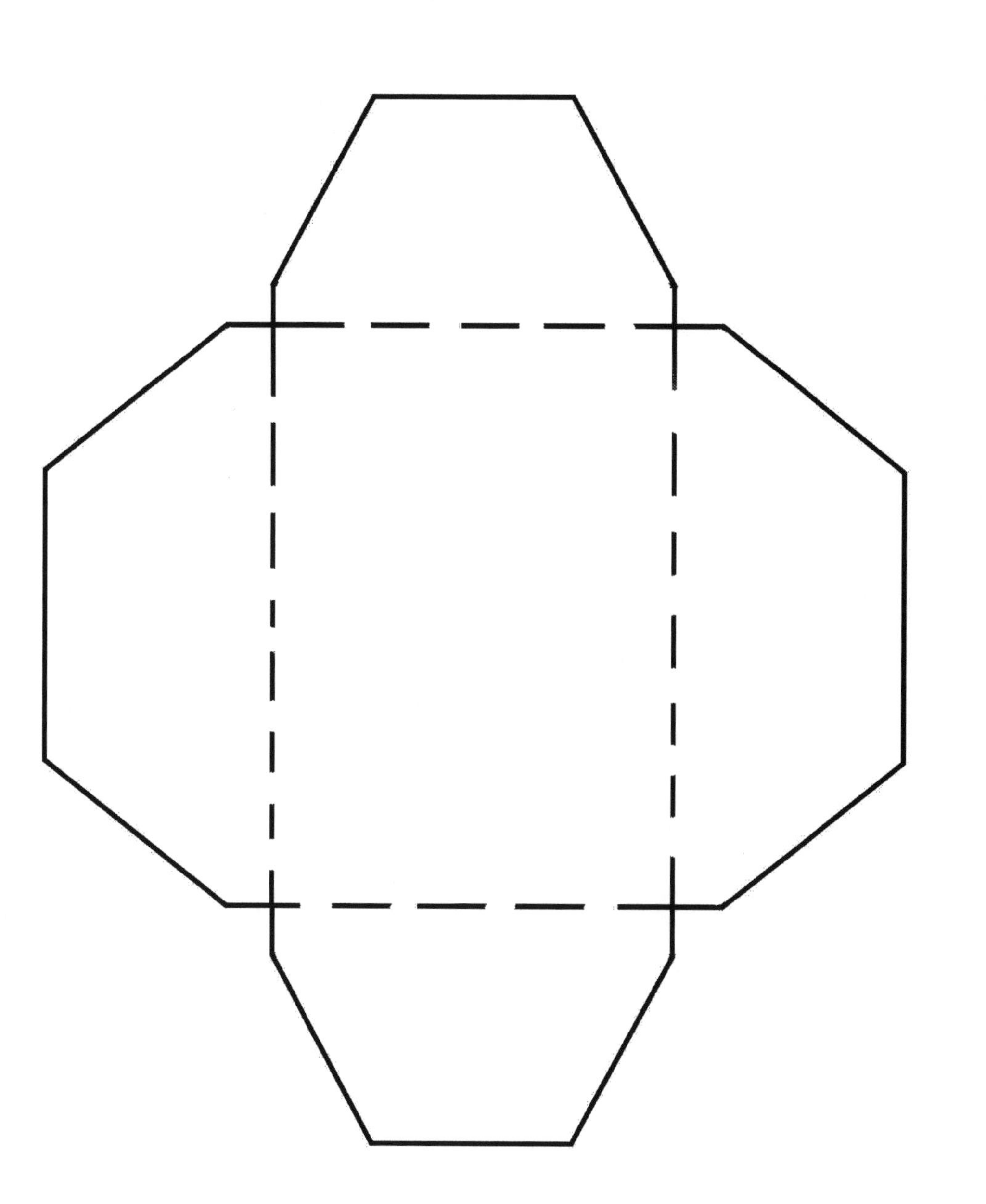

Pineapple Coconut Cake

1/2 can of milk

1/2 cup of sugar

1/4 cup of butter

2 eggs

1 can of coconut

1 can of sliced pineapples.

1 cup of self-rising flour.

Add ingredients together. Could vary.

Bake to taste

Add pineapple

Sprinkle Coconut.

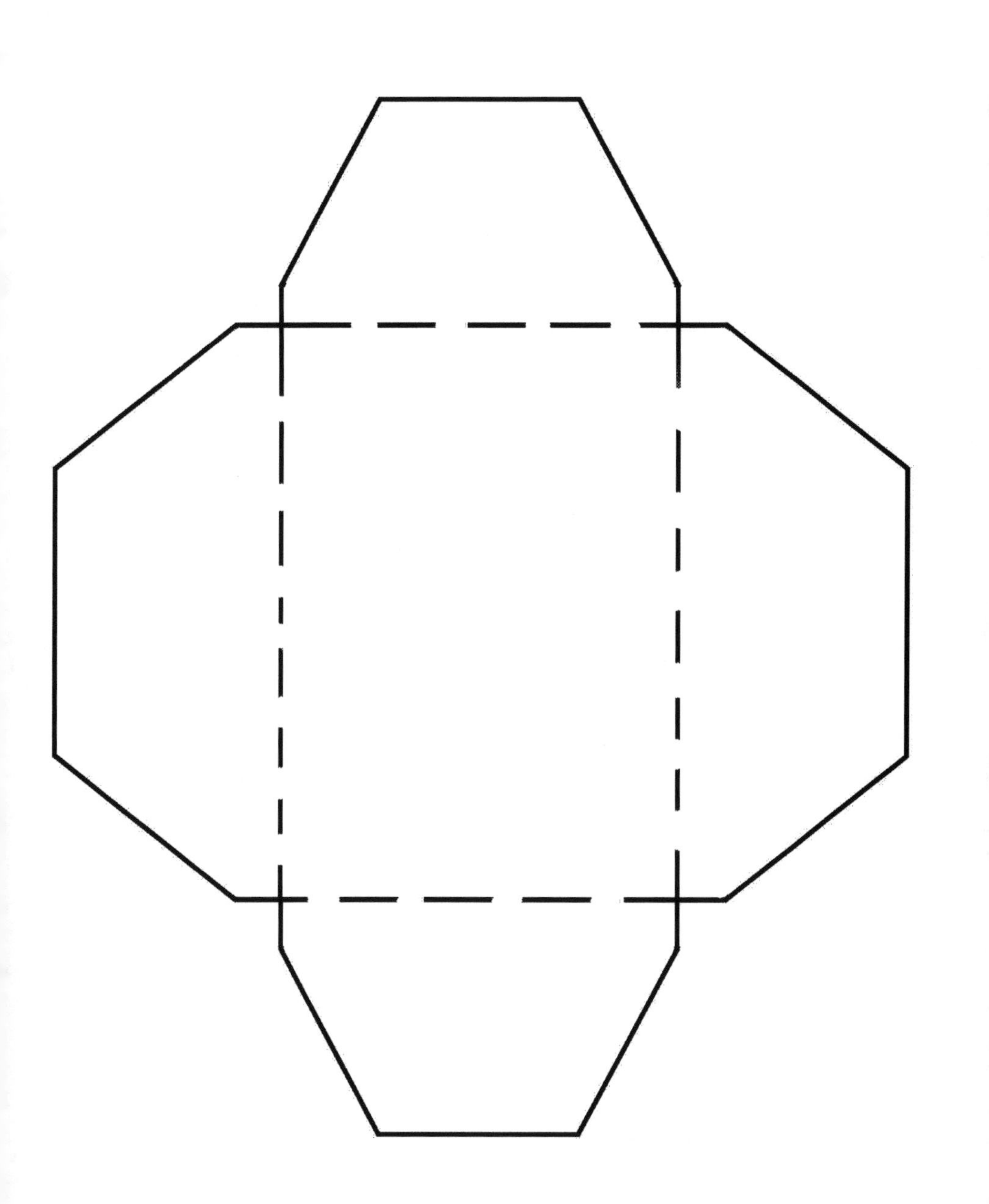

I am a unique and inspiring woman,
As long as I have education as my tool,
I believe I will be swimming on the right pool.

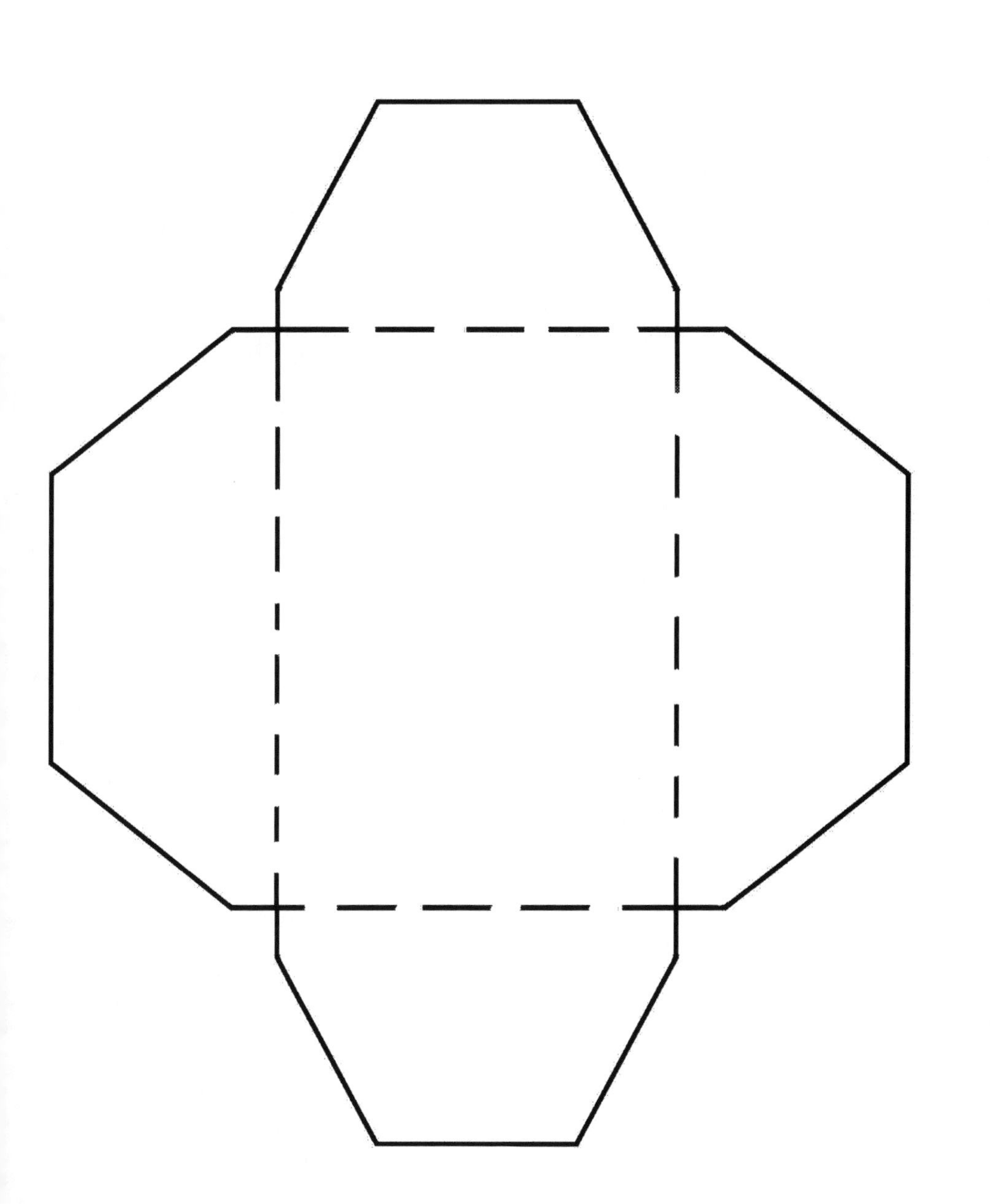

Chicken Salad

1 lb chicken baked and sliced

1/2 lb lettuce

1 small tomato

French/Ranch or mayo dressing

Combine chicken, lettuce, tomato together.

Top with dressing.

Good meal made well.

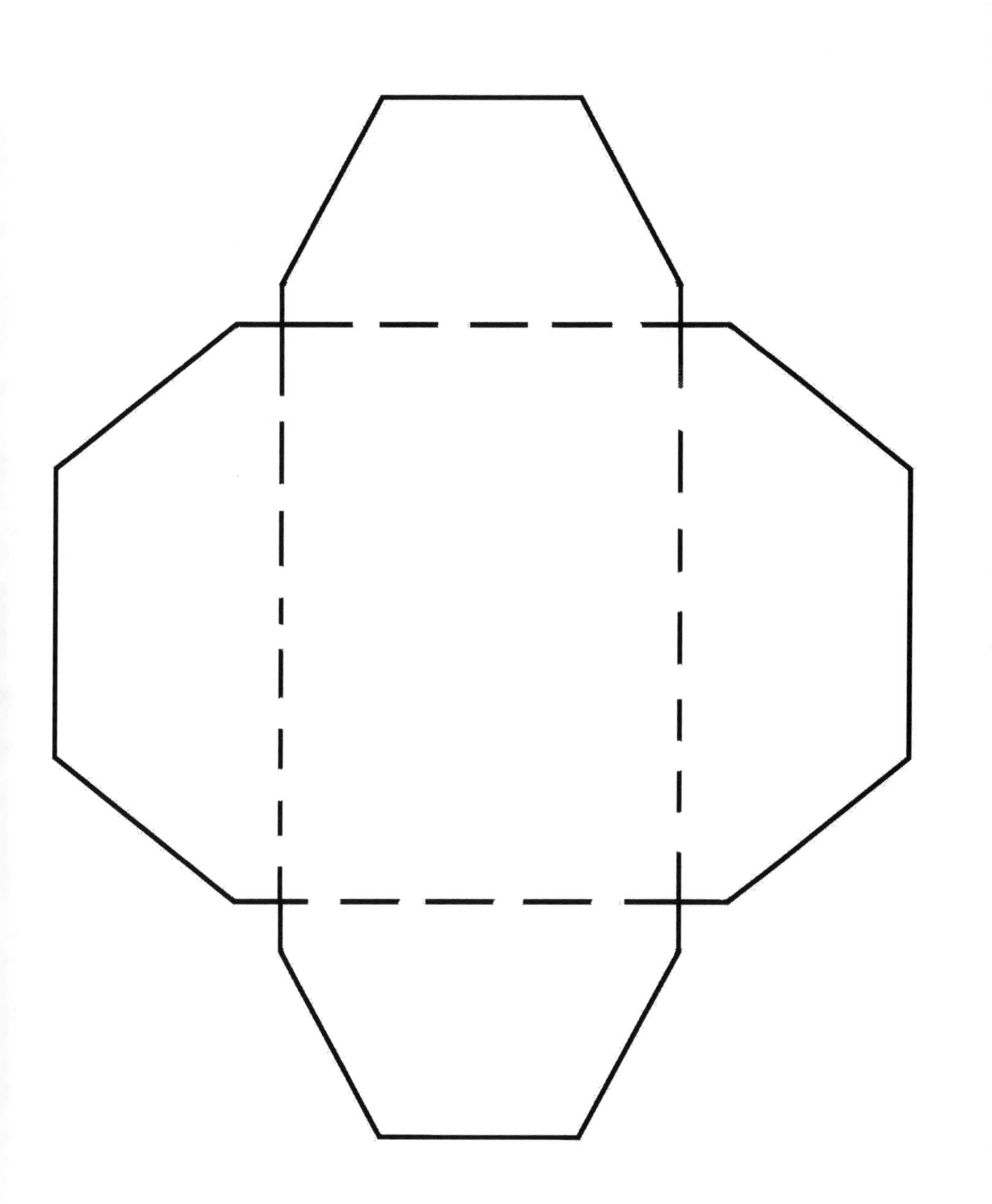

My Favorite Karaoke song

This Will be by Natalie Cole

What's Going On by Marvin Gaye

You Rock My World by Michael Jackson

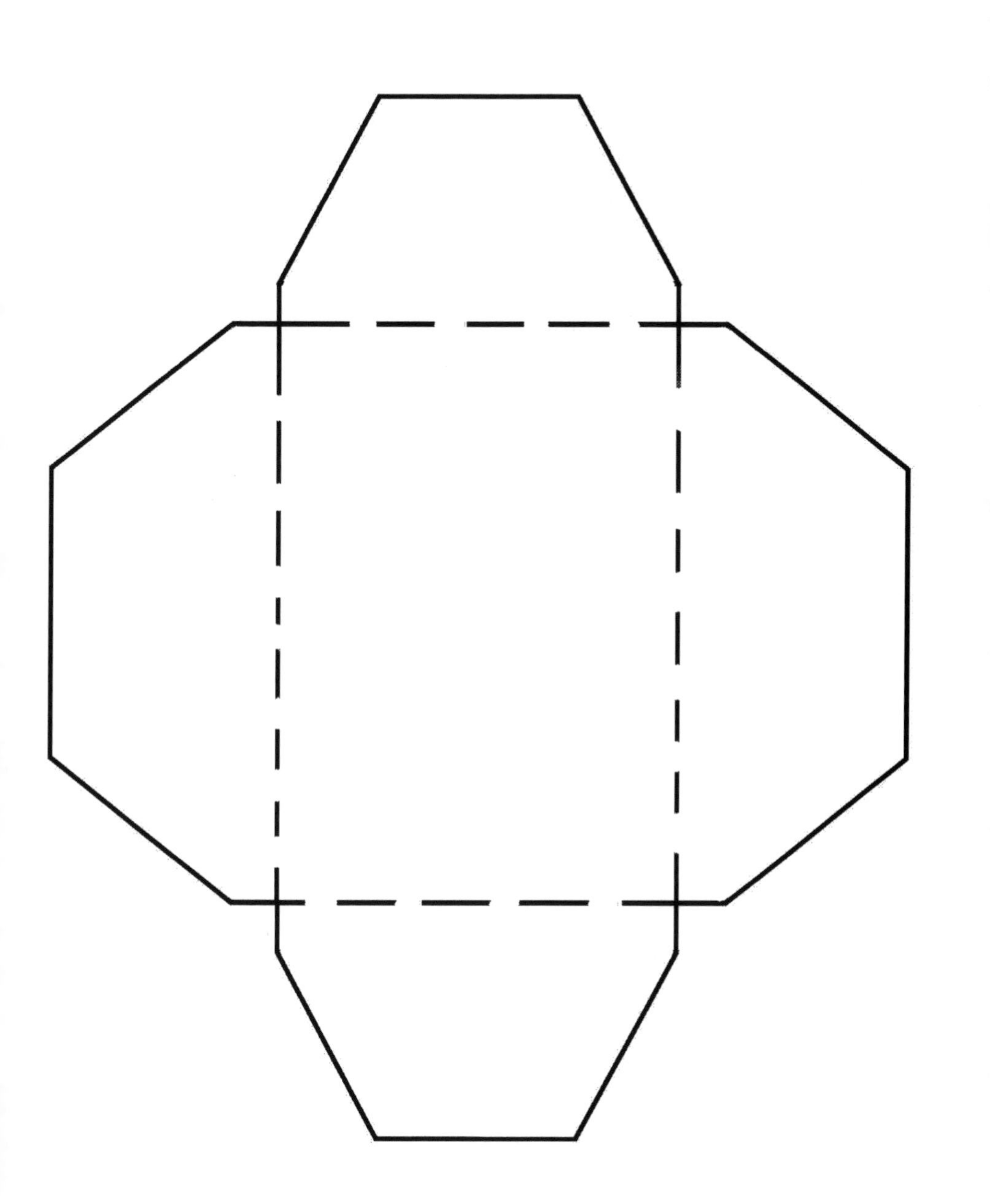

Cheers to your own song in life!

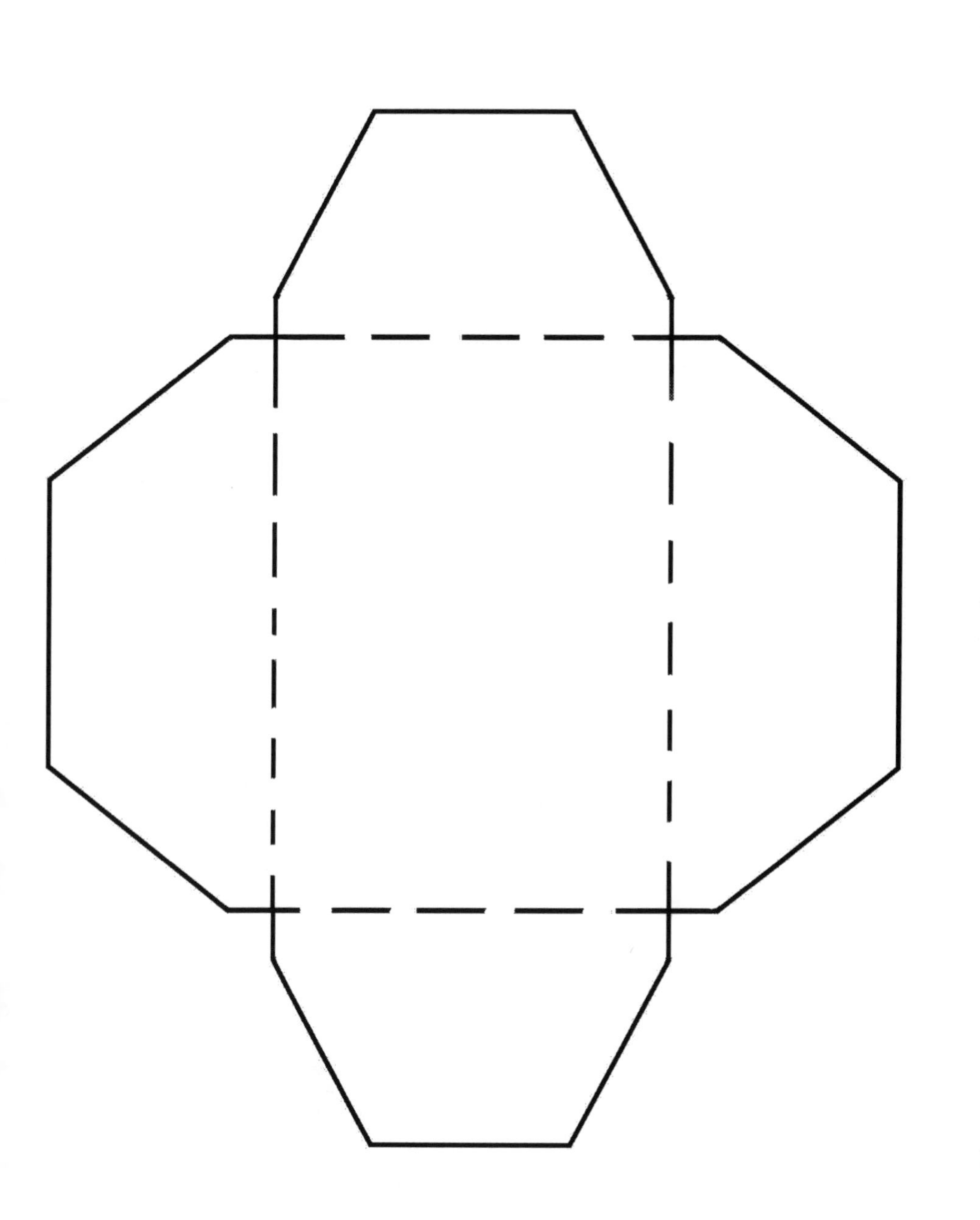

Thank you to all. Live, love and learn.

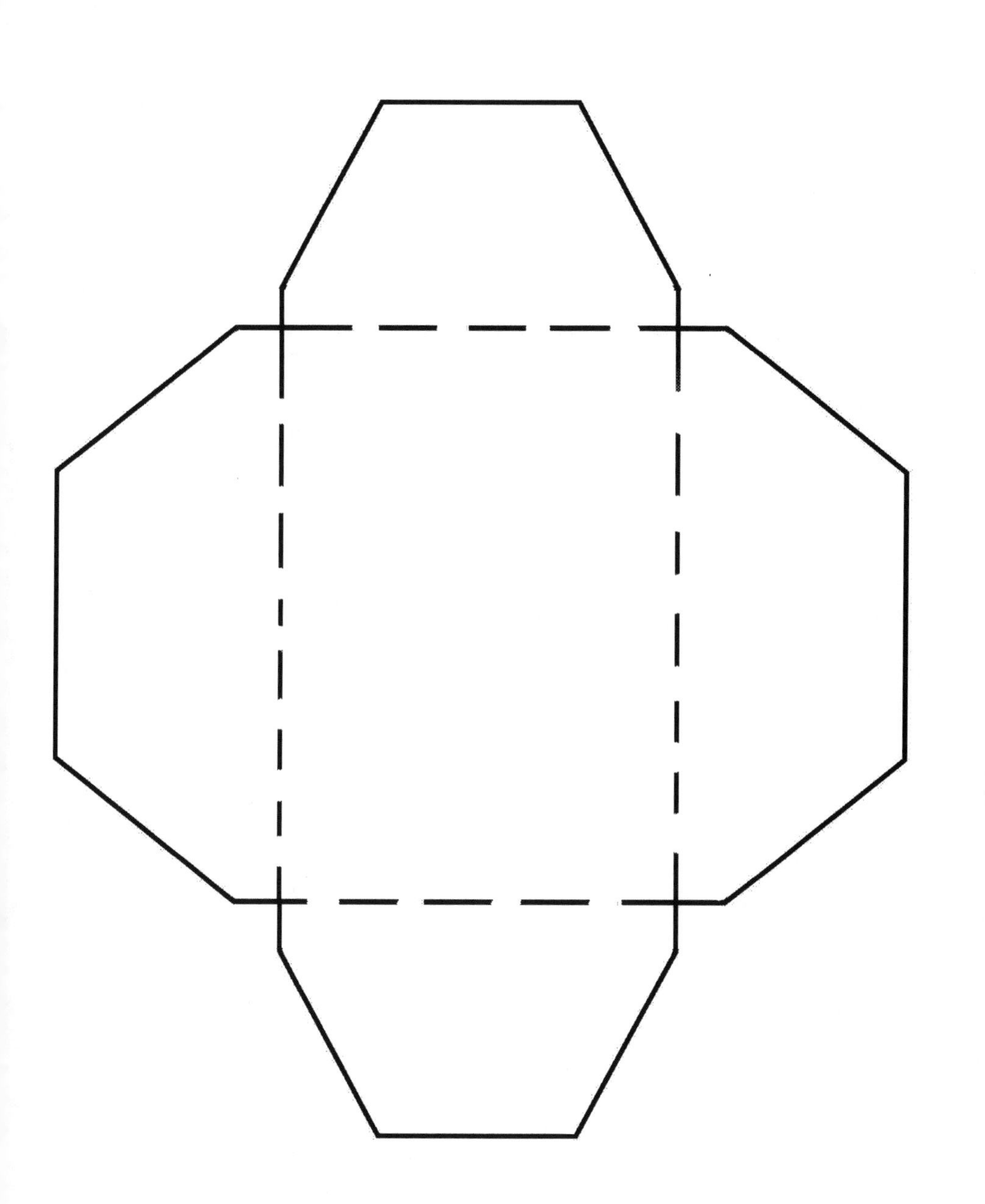

Thank you

This book is dedicated to the ones I love.

SPECIAL AWARD
MAGIC
MAILERS
BOOK
by
SUGAR DIAMOND
PRINCESS QUEEN
SPECIAL AWARD

Printed in the United States
By Bookmasters